◄ *the* ►
PRACTICAL
WITCH'S
GUIDED JOURNAL

for Wisdom, Healing, and Self-Love

CERRIDWEN GREENLEAF

Illustrations by
MARA PENNY

RP STUDIO
PHILADELPHIA

RP Studio™
Hachette Book Group
1290 Avenue of the Americas, New York, NY 10104
www.runningpress.com
@Running_Press

Printed in China

First Edition: April 2020

Published by RP Studio, an imprint of Perseus Books, LLC, a subsidiary of Hachette Book
Group, Inc. The RP Studio name and logo is a trademark of the Hachette Book Group.

The publisher is not responsible for websites (or their content)
that are not owned by the publisher.

Design by Susan Van Horn.

ISBN: 978-0-7624-6958-1

1010

10 9 8 7 6 5 4 3 2

Focus your attention on the natural world.
How do you stay attuned with nature?

_____
_____
_____
_____
_____
_____
_____
_____
_____
_____
_____
_____
_____
_____
_____
_____
_____
_____
_____
_____
_____

Where is the best place for pensive reflection?

How do you find inner peace?

What do you do to bless your home?

_____

_____

_____

_____

_____

_____

_____

_____

_____

_____

_____

_____

_____

_____

_____

_____

_____

_____

_____

_____

_____

_____

FIVE-MINUTE MAGIC

To anoint your home as a sacred space and protect you from harm, rub any one of the following essential oils, undiluted, on your front door at the top and bottom: cinnamon, clove, cypress, dragon's blood, or frankincense. Walk through the door and close it securely. Take the remaining essential oil and anoint every other door and window. At the witching hour of midnight, light anointed white candles and place them in every doorway and windowsill.

Meditation is a simple yet powerful ritual.
How can you meditate in your daily life and stay
connected to the earth?

Who inspires you? Why?

Wish good fortune
on friends and family.

Protect yourself from negative energy here.

_____

_____

_____

_____

_____

_____

_____

_____

_____

_____

_____

_____

_____

_____

_____

_____

_____

_____

_____

_____

FIVE-MINUTE MAGIC

For dispelling negative energy, plant heather, hawthorn, holly, hyacinth, hyssop, ivy, juniper, periwinkle, and nasturtiums. For healing, plant sage, wood sorrel, carnation, onion, garlic, peppermint, and rosemary. Farming and working with plants are guided by the moon and should take place during the waxing moon in the sign of Taurus.

Looking for a relationship? Record your love potion here and you may find a new relationship faster than you think.

_____

_____

_____

_____

_____

_____

_____

_____

_____

_____

PRACTICAL WITCH'S SPELL

If you are looking for love, perform this rite and you will soon find a lover to satisfy your needs. On the night of the next new moon, take two pieces of rose quartz and place them on the floor in the center of your bedroom. Light two red candles and use this affirming chant:

Beautiful crystal I hold this night,

Flame with love for my delight,

Goddess of Love, I ask of you,

Guide me in the path that is true.

Harm to none as love comes to me.

This I ask and so it shall be.

Reflect on a time your magic helped someone.

Amulets are the perfect way to show a loved one that you care. Who could you offer this special gift to?

_____
_____
_____
_____
_____
_____
_____
_____
_____
_____
_____
_____
_____
_____
_____
_____

FIVE-MINUTE MAGIC

If you create amulets to share with friends and loved ones, your good intention will be returned many times over. Make your amulet by stuffing a muslin drawstring bag with dried herbs. Keep these amulets with you at all times, in a pocket or a purse, or on a string or a chain around your neck.

FOR COURAGE: *Mullein, borage flowers*

DEPRESSION AID: *Nettle, yarrow*

TO RECOGNIZE OTHER WITCHES: *Ivy, rue, agrimony, broomstraw, maidenhair fern*

FOR SAFE TRAVEL: *Comfrey*

FOR FERTILITY: *Mistletoe, cyclamen*

FOR PROTECTION FROM DECEIT: *Snapdragon*

FOR GOOD HEALTH: *Rue*

FOR SUCCESS: *Woodruff*

FOR STRENGTH: *Mugwort*

FOR YOUTH: *An acorn*

Sketch your altar.
What does it hold and how does it represent you?

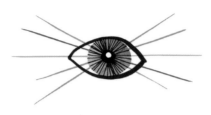

Open your third eye. What would you like to understand more clearly in your life?

What makes you happy?

_____

_____

_____

_____

_____

_____

_____

_____

_____

_____

_____

_____

_____

_____

_____

_____

_____

_____

_____

_____

_____

_____

_____

_____
_____
_____
_____
_____
_____
_____
_____
_____
_____
_____
_____

FIVE-MINUTE MAGIC

We recommend doing this sanctuary spell at least once a year, as it imbues your home—your sacred space—with an aura of serenity and makes the blessings in your life tangible. Sit in a comfortable position with your absolute favorite essential-oil-scented candle lit and placed in a bowl in front of you. Surround yourself with your favorite crystals. Think about the blessings and gifts in your life. What are you grateful for at this moment? There is a powerful magic in recognizing all that you possess and in maintaining an attitude of gratitude. Breathe steadily and deeply, inhaling and exhaling slowly for five minutes. As you meditate, send the positive energy into your crystals and the flame of the candle. Now, the blessings are there in the bowl any time you need them.

What are your hopes and intentions for the present and future?

_____

_____

_____

_____

_____

_____

_____

_____

_____

_____

PRACTICAL WITCH'S SPELL

Write your intention on paper and place an anointed candle in a candleholder. Light it, and say:

Blessed candle, light of the Goddess,

I burn this light of [deity's name].

Hear my prayer, O [deity's name], hear my need.

Grant my wish and give me hope.

Do so with all your grace,

And magical speed.

Now read your intention as you wrote it on the paper. Roll the paper into a scroll and, using a few drops of the warm wax from your intention candle, seal your sacred statement. Place the paper on your altar or in a special place where it can be safe until your intention is realized.

There are many kinds of crystals that can help
you on your journey through life. What are your favorites
and which do you need in your life?

Design a charm bracelet that represents your wishes for the future.

What tools do you find essential for making magic?

How do you dispel unwanted stress?

PRACTICAL WITCH'S SPELL

When you are feeling unwell, stressed, or fatigued, or when you have a case of the blues, dose yourself with a teaspoon or dropper of one of the following floral essence remedies:

ANXIETY:
Garlic, rosemary, aspen, periwinkle, lemon balm,
white chestnut, gentian

DEPRESSION:
Borage, sunflower, larch, chamomile, geranium, yerba santa,
black cohosh, lavender, mustard

EXHAUSTION:
Aloe, yarrow, olive, sweet chestnut

LETHARGY:
Aloe, thyme, peppermint

STRESS:
Dill, echinacea, thyme, mistletoe, lemon balm

After you have taken the medicine, chant these words aloud:

May I be healed by root and flower,

May I become well through Mother Nature's power.

May sleep and strength return to me,

I am now healthy, happy, and stress-free.

With harm to none. So mote it be.

Is there a specific deity with whom you feel an affinity?

_____

_____

_____

_____

_____

_____

_____

_____

_____

_____

_____

_____

_____

_____

_____

_____

_____

_____

FIVE-MINUTE MAGIC

Dandelion root tea can call upon the spirit of anyone whose advice you might need. What deity can assist you now in your life? Simply place a freshly brewed tea, using this root, on your bedroom altar or nightstand. Before you sleep, say the name of your helper deity aloud seven times. In a dream or vision, the spirit will visit you and answer all your questions.

Record your favorite spells for a happy, healthy life.

What items would be helpful to use in your spellwork?

Is there a certain phase of the moon that helps bring you clarity?

_____

_____

_____

_____

_____

_____

_____

_____

_____

_____

_____

_____

PRACTICAL WITCH'S SPELL

When the new moon is in an air sign—Aquarius, Gemini, or Libra—
light the following incenses: lavender and sandalwood. Light one
white candle and one blue candle and say:

Winged Mercury, God of air,

I entreat you to bring me sight and true awareness.

Like the wind, speed my way.

Make everything new.

This spell should give you sharpness and great clarity of mind.
Listen to your intuition now; it will not fail you. Write down your
insights in your Book of Shadows.

Charm boxes or spell boxes are very important for storing sacred objects. What do you include in yours?

Dispel your fears here.

Design a pendulum to guide you
through important decisions.

PRACTICAL WITCH'S SPELL

Many witches carry a pendulum with them to help make decisions. Take a strong string or length of leather and tie a ring, gemstone, or crystal to the end. By the light of the new moon, take a bundle of sage, light one end, and pass the smoke over your pendulum, smudging and purifying your space. Holding the pendulum still, chant:

Guide me to the path of truth,

Goddess hear my song.

This pendulum I charge with my energy,

To judge right from wrong.

So mote it be.

Any time you need advice before making a decision, dangle the pendulum and observe its movement. Swaying from front to back means *yes*, left to right means *no*.

List your favorite gems and crystals.
What do you use them for?

_____

_____

_____

_____

_____

_____

_____

_____

_____

_____

_____

_____

_____

FIVE-MINUTE MAGIC

Keep a magic wishing box on your desk. Every so often, look at it and make a wish upon your heart's desire. It's easy to make: Take a bowl or an empty box and fill it halfway with sand. Place these suggested wish stones in any arrangement you find pleasing.

AGATE *for a new home*

AMETHYST *for spirituality*

CARNELIAN or **LAPIS LAZULI** *for a new job*

CORAL *for wanting children*

FOOL'S GOLD *for money*

ROSE QUARTZ *for love*

Plan a magical week. What spells and candles will you use?

_____

_____

_____

_____

_____

_____

_____

_____

_____

_____

_____

_____

_____

_____

_____

_____

_____

_____

_____

Project your positive energy here.

_____

_____

_____

_____

_____

_____

_____

_____

_____

_____

PRACTICAL WITCH'S SPELL

The ultimate magic is to generate positive energy that spirals out-
ward, improving everything in its path. You can contribute to
universal peace and healing by burning a white candle anointed
with rose oil on your altar during a waning moon on Woden's Day
(Wednesday). Place a single white rose in water, and lay a bundle of
dried white sage beside rose incense. Light the incense, then take
the sage bundle, light the end, and pass the smoke over your altar to
smudge the space. Chant:

War and grief will come to an end,

We walk the path of peace,

Love thy neighbor as thy self,

All we need is love.

With harm to none, only understanding.

What is your favorite season?
How can you reflect this in your altar?

What colors are you drawn to and how do you
use them in your ritual work?

It's always important to express gratitude.
Count your blessings here.

PRACTICAL WITCH'S SPELL

Sit in a comfortable position in front of your serenity altar and meditate. Think about your blessings. What are you grateful for at this moment? There is a powerful magic in recognizing all that you possess. Breathe steadily and deeply, inhaling and exhaling slowly for twenty minutes. Then chant:

Great Goddess, giver of all the fruits of this earth,

Of all bounty, beauty, and well-being,

Bless all who give and receive these gifts.

I am made of sacred earth, purest water,

Sacred fire and wildest wind.

Blessing upon me. Blessing upon thee,

Mother Earth and Sister Sky.

So mote it be.

_____

_____

_____

_____

_____

_____

_____

_____

_____

_____

_____

How do you charge your spellwork with healing energy?

PRACTICAL WITCH'S SPELL

Place 1 quart of rough sea salt or Epsom salt in a large bowl. Add the juice of two freshly squeezed lemons, ½ cup of sesame oil, and 4 drops each of lavender and jasmine oils. Stir until well mixed. When your tub is one-third full, add one-quarter of the salt mixture under the faucet. Breathe in deeply and proclaim:

Remove from me anything impure,

Of heart, spirit, and mind.

My wish is to once again become whole,

Free of pain and sadness,

And filled with all that is better in me.

When the tub is full, step inside and repeat the prayer; use the rest of the salt to gently massage your body.

How can you add more joy and enchantment
to your daily life?

Record your favorite spells for uplifting your spirit
and nourishing your soul.

What spells help you relax?

What's your astrological sign? Does it ring true?

What do you grow in your herb garden?
Create a sketch of it here.

_____

_____

_____

_____

_____

_____

_____

_____

_____

_____

_____

_____

_____

_____

_____

_____

_____

FIVE-MINUTE MAGIC

The following list of herbs can be used in any ritual work in which the intention is prosperity: allspice, almond, basil, bergamot, mint, cedar, cinnamon, cinquefoil, clover, dill, ginger, heliotrope, honey-suckle, hyssop, jasmine, myrtle, nutmeg, oak moss, sassafras, vervain, and woodruff. Try these alone or in mixtures, tinctures, or ground into your incenses. You can also plant a prosperity garden and refresh your abundance altar with herbs and flowers grown by your own hand.

How can you use your magic for good?

What is your flower power?

PRACTICAL WITCH'S SPELL

This flower-infused potpourri is wonderful for clearing the way for the new in your life and planting "seeds" for new moon beginnings. Flower ingredients:

Rose

Snapdragon

Marigold

Carnation

Cyclamen

Place the flowers in a bowl and then sprinkle them with a few drops of geranium, clove, and cinnamon oil. Place the mixture on the south point of your altar for the duration of a full lunar cycle, from new moon to new moon.

Sketch a design for a new wand.
What crystals would you use?

How do you incorporate spiritual
practices into your busy life?

What do you keep in your Book of Shadows?

Conjure the energy that you desire in your life.

_____

_____

_____

_____

_____

_____

_____

_____

_____

_____

_____

PRACTICAL WITCH'S SPELL

To help center yourself, light a candle and meditate on it. By focusing on the flame, you bring your being and awareness into focus. Light your favorite meditation incense. Scratch your name into the candle. Next, scratch your hope onto the candle. Light your candle and recite:

This candle burns for me.

Here burns my hope for [say what you are hoping for].

Here burns the flame of insight,

May I see clearly in this new light.

Sit with your eyes closed for a few minutes and picture yourself realizing your most heartfelt hopes and truest desires.

Record your spiritual intentions here.

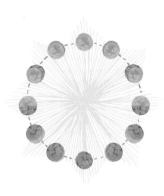

What phase of the moon speaks to you?

How do you observe the sabbats?

Record the plants that help you heal during a time of need.

Herbal teas and brews can help calm any storm.
What herbs create the perfect brew?

_____

_____

_____

_____

_____

_____

_____

_____

_____

_____

_____

_____

_____

_____

_____

_____

_____

_____

_____

_____

_____

_____

_____

_____

_____

_____

_____

PRACTICAL WITCH'S SPELL

No matter what astrological sign or moon phase, witches' brews can improve your life. Tea conjures a very powerful alchemy because when you drink it, you take the magic inside. For an ambrosial brew, add a sliver of gingerroot and a pinch each of chamomile and peppermint to a cup of hot black tea. Before you drink, pray:

This day I pray for calm, for health,

And the wisdom to see the beauty of each waking moment.

Blessings abound.

So mote it be.

What flower medicines have you used?

Record some of your most recent research for rituals and lore.

Try to catch a fallen leaf—it's the best kind of luck!
Draw a picture of your magical leaf here.

_____

_____

_____

_____

_____

_____

_____

_____

_____

_____

_____

_____

_____

PRACTICAL WITCH'S SPELL

A lucky charm for solvency is to take seven seeds and put them on your windowsill during a full moon for seven hours. Pick up the moon-charged seeds, and while holding them in the palm of your hand, speak this wish-spell:

Luck be quick, luck be kind.

And by lucky seven, good luck will be mine.

Plant these lucky seeds well and be on the lookout for blessings to shower down upon you. You might receive a gift, win free services, or unexpectedly find money.

What spices do you use in your ritual work
and what do you use them for?

Make a list of your favorite magical recipes.